Start Maths
ON OUR WAY

# Numbers

**Ann Montague-Smith**

QED Publishing

2 + 3 + 1 = 6



First published in the UK in 2004 by
QED Publishing
A Quarto Group Company
226 City Road
London, EC1V 2TT

www.qed-publishing.co.uk



A Catalogue record for this book is available from the British Library.

ISBN 978 1 84835 133 2

Written by Ann Montague-Smith
Designed and edited by The Complete Works
Illustrated by Jenny Tulip
Photography by Steve Lumb and Michael Wicks

Creative Director Louise Morley
Editorial Manager Jean Coppendale

Printed and bound in China

With thanks to: ELC

# Contents

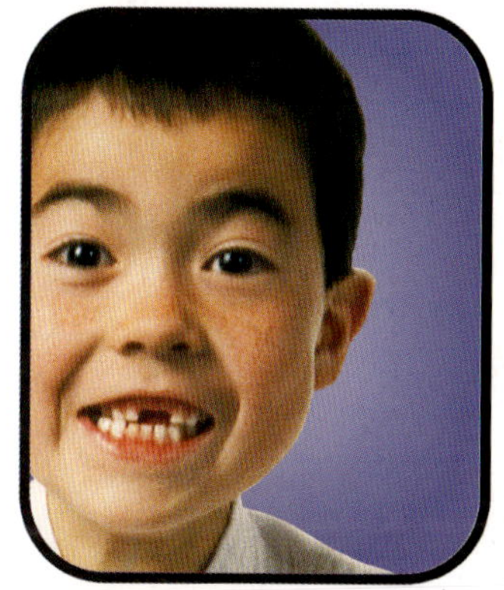

# 1 more and 1 fewer

5 people are on the bus. 1 more gets on.
How many are on the bus now?

At the next bus stop, 8 people are now on the bus. 1 gets off. How many are left on the bus?

$$4 + 1 + 1 = 6$$

## Challenge

Ask a friend to count a small handful of bricks. Say, 'What if there was 1 more or 1 fewer. How many then?'

2 + 3 + 1 = 6

# Adding 2 sets

How many doughnuts can you see?
How many scones are there?
How many doughnuts and scones are there altogether?

How many muffins and smiley faces are there altogether?

## Challenge

Use some plasticine.
Make some doughnuts
and iced buns.
How many doughnuts
are there?
How many iced buns?
How many cakes
have you made
altogether?

# Adding 3 sets

How many hats, scarves and coats can you see in each set?
How many hats, scarves and coats altogether?

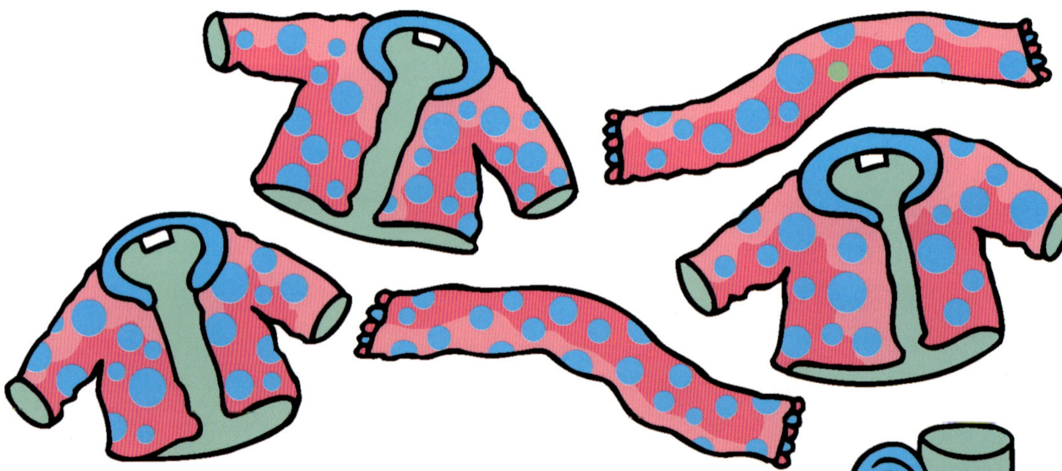

Which set has the largest total of hats, scarves and coats? Which set has the smallest total?

# 4 + 1 + 1 = 6

## Challenge

Draw 3 different sets of clothes. How many clothes are there in each set? How many clothes have you drawn altogether?

# Counting on

Play this game with friends. You will each need a counter for the track. You will also need a counter for the spinner. Throw a counter onto the spinner. Move that number on the track. The first one to reach 10 is the winner.

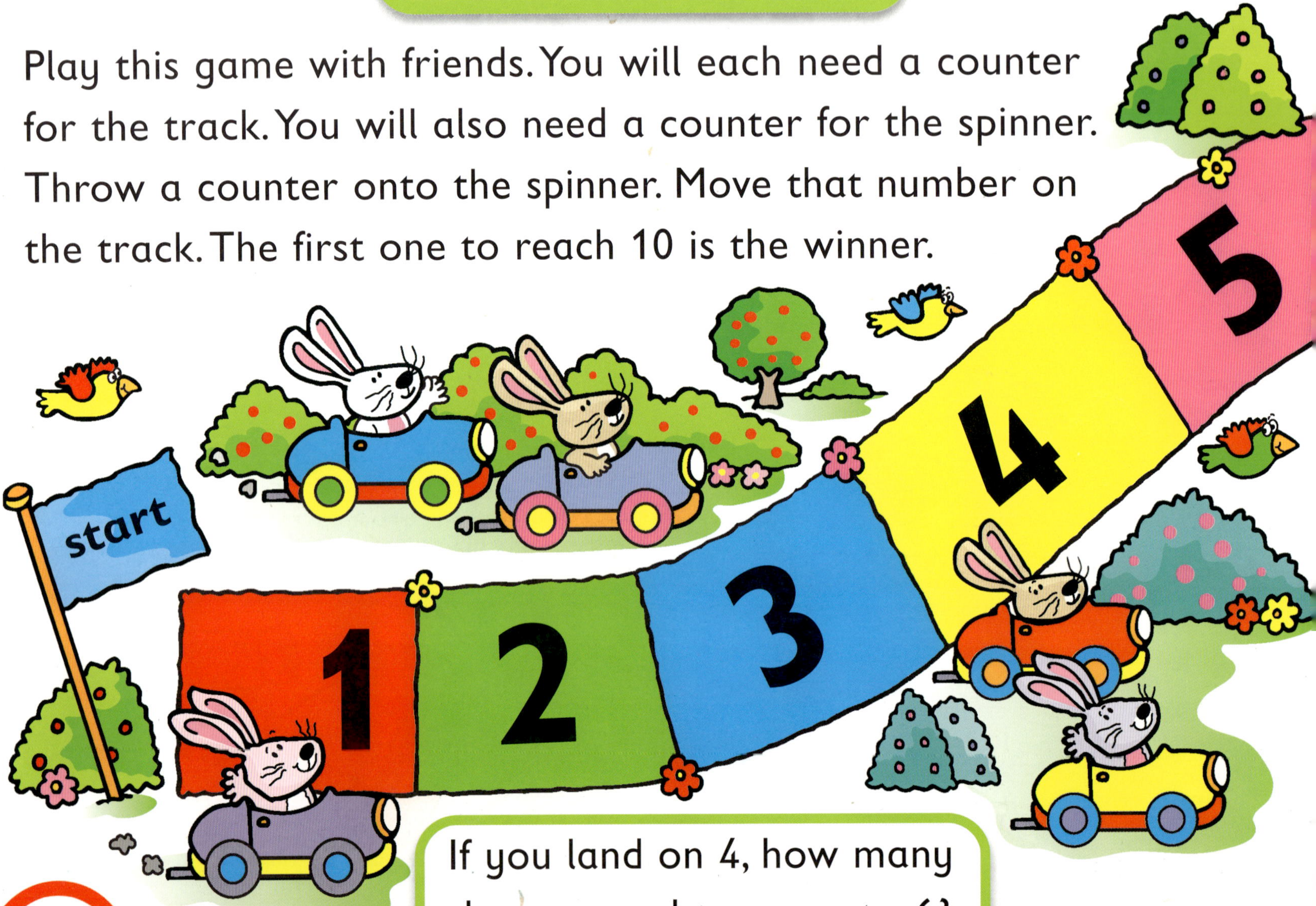


If you land on 4, how many do you need to move to 6?

## Challenge

Play the game again. This time use a 1 to 6 dice. You will need to throw the exact number you need to win.

What number did you start on?
What number are you on now?
So how many did you count on?

# Hiding a quantity

The magician has put 3 rabbits into the hat.
Now he puts 1 more rabbit into the hat.
How many rabbits are in the hat altogether?

The magician has 4 rabbits in the hat. He puts 2 more in. How many are there altogether now?

$$4 + 1 + 1 = 6$$

## Challenge

Put some counters into a bag and say how many. Take some more and ask a friend to count them. Put these into the bag too. Now ask, 'How many counters are there in the bag?'

# Making totals

Find 2 sets of space bugs which total 6.

How many different ways can you find to total 6?

Can you find 2 sets which total 5?

4 + 1 + 1 = 6

## Challenge

Can you find 2 sets of space bugs which total 7?
Can you find a different way to do this?
Which set gets left out?

# Count what is left

See if you can work out what is left.

Martha eats 4 jellies.
How many are left?

Desi eats 1 cake.
How many are left?

# 4 + 1 + 1 = 6

## Challenge

Take 6 counters and hide some under a cup. Show how many are left. Ask a friend, 'How many counters are hidden?'

Tom eats 2 biscuits. How many are left?

Anna eats 2 lollipops. How many are left?

# Shopping

Get 10 play money coins.
Choose a toy. Put the correct number of coins on that toy.
How much did you spend?
How many coins have you got left?

2

4

10

6

5

Take the coins off. Now buy another toy.
How many coins have you got left now?

## Challenge

Choose 2 toys to buy.
How much did they cost?
How many coins have
you got left?
Can you find different
ways to do this?

# I know about totals to 10

Put 1 counter onto each treasure chest. You and a friend will each need a counter. Take turns to roll a dice. Move that number of spaces. If you land on a treasure chest, take the counter. The winner is the one who takes the most counters.

How many counters have you got? How many has your friend got? How many counters are there altogether?

## Challenge

Play the game again with 10 counters each. Every time you land on a treasure chest, put a counter onto the chest. Say how many counters you have now. The winner is the first person with no counters left.

# Supporting notes for adults

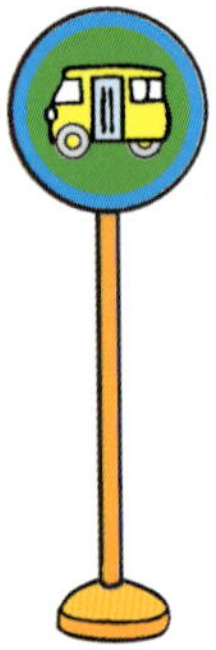

### 1 more and 1 fewer – pages 4-5

If the children cannot yet count on 1, suggest to them that they use the line of flower pots to count on 1 more, or back 1. Suggest other amounts of people on the bus, with 1 more or 1 fewer, such as 6 people, 4 people… up to 9 people.

### Adding 2 sets – pages 6-7

Ask the children to combine different sets of cakes. They can count one set, then count the second set. Finally, they can count all of those cakes to find the total. Encourage them over time to count on from the second set: 3 add 2 is 3 and 4, 5.

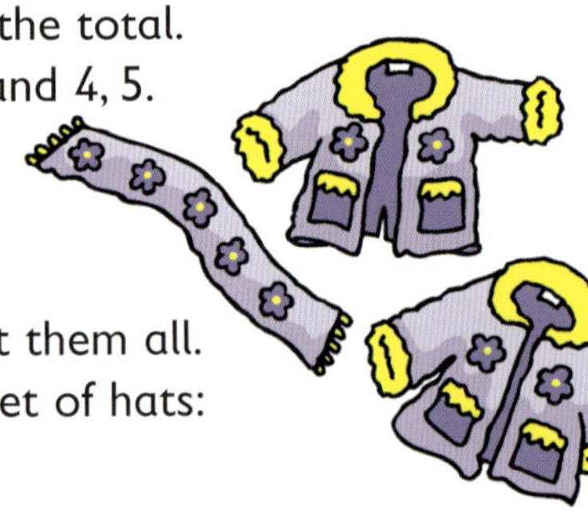

### Adding 3 sets – pages 8-9

The children may find it easier at this stage to count each set, then to count them all. Encourage them over time to count on mentally from the total of the first set of hats: 2 add 1 add 2 is 2 and 3 and 4, 5.

### Counting on – pages 10-11

Ask the children to say what number they must move their counter to by asking them to count on in their heads. If they find this difficult, let them count on by moving their counter along the track, then together count on mentally: start on 4, spinner number of 2 so 4, 5, 6.

4 + 1 + 1 = 6

## Hiding a quantity – pages 12-13

Encourage the children to count on from the quantity that is hidden in the hat. If they find this difficult, count together. Suggest other numbers of rabbits in the hat, and to be added to them. Keep the totals up to 6 to begin with.

## Making totals – pages 14-15

If children find this activity hard, give them 8 counters and ask them to make 2 sets in different ways. Then try the activity on the page again.

## Count what is left – pages 16-17

Encourage the children to count all of the pieces of food in the picture, then to count the ones that have been eaten. If they cannot say how many are left, suggest that they cover those that have been eaten with a counter, and count those they can still see.

## Shopping – pages 18-19

Encourage the children to count out the coins for each toy and say how much that is. Then they can count how many coins are left. Encourage them to put this into a number sentence: 'I have 10 coins; my drum cost 3 coins; now I have 7 coins left'.

## I know about totals to 10 – pages 20-21

Ask questions such as, 'How many counters have you got? How many has … got? So how many counters have you got altogether? How many more are there still on the board?'

# Suggestions for using this book

Children will enjoy looking through the book and talking about the colourful pictures. Sit somewhere comfortable together. Please read the instructions to the children, then encourage them to take part in the activity and check whether or not they have understood what to do.

In this book, children are encouraged to work practically to solve addition and subtraction problems. They are introduced to the strategy of counting on from a quantity in order to find a total. For example, when adding 3 and 5 they could begin by counting the five: 1, 2, 3, 4, 5. Now they count on from 5 for three more: 6, 7, 8. So 8 is the total. At first, children will count on from either quantity. You may wish to gently suggest that they try counting on from the smaller quantity. Then try it the other way round. They will, of course, find the result is the same. Suggest now that they try counting on from the larger quantity. This is an easier way to do it!

Similarly, children can use the counting on strategy for subtraction. They can count on from the smaller quantity to reach the larger. So, in a problem such as, 'There are 5 biscuits. Tom eats 2. How many are left?' the children can count on from 2 to 5, keeping a tally with their fingers.

Shopping using coins is introduced. Use play money coins worth '1' unit each to begin with. Children can then use counting to show what they spend and how much money is left.